In 1624, when Louis XIII inaugurated his modest château, built on a hill in the midst of forests west of Paris, there was nothing to suggest the remarkable destiny awaiting Versailles. At the beginning of his reign, Louis XIV himself did not suspect that he would change his father's château into the greatest palace in the western world, adorned with superb gardens and surrounded by a royal city. Louis XV and Louis XVI showed concern for the protection of the inheritance left by the Sun King, while at the same time enriching and partially altering it.

Nearly two centuries of persistent effort were needed to create one of the highlights of our civilization on the former marshes of Versailles. It looked as if the Revolution would compromise everything, but suddenly Versailles no longer seemed the very symbol of the absolute monarchy and nearly everything was saved. A revelation had taken place: France had understood that generations of artists had left her an incomparable cultural heritage.

As their creator had wished, these treasures are still there for visitors of this planet, to be admired and loved by them.

In this way, the Château de Versailles, whose orientation, construction and decoration were inspired by the myth of the Sun and Apollo, will continue to reflect the radiating splendour of French classicism and will always be a privileged meeting-place for the inheritors of the most noble traditions and the truest representatives of the modern world.

CONTENTS

PHOTOGRAPHIES DE JACQUES GIRARD JEAN-CLAUDE VARGA ET RENÉ-PAUL PAYEN
COMPOSITIONS GRAPHIQUES ET MAQUETTE DE PIERRE BÉQUET
PHOTOCOMPOSITION ET PHOTOGRAVURE BUSSIÈRE ARTS GRAPHIQUES, PARIS
ACHEVÉ D'IMPRIMER PAR LES FILS DE F. LESCURE, IMPRIMEURS A PARIS, MAI 1985
COPYRIGHT BY ÉDITIONS D'ART LYS 1985. DÉPOT LÉGAL 2ᵉᵐᵉ TRIMESTRE 1985.

End-papers:
games held by Louis XV
◀ in the Hall of Mirrors in 1747.

LOUIS XIV VISITING THE
MONTBAURON RESERVOIRS,
PAINTING BY J.B. MARTIN ▶

VERSAILLES

COMPLETE TOUR

commentary by

GERALD VAN DER KEMP

Member of the Institute
Honorary General Inspector of National Museums

Translation by Bronia Fuchs.

1624 Louis XIII orders a hunting pavilion to be built on the small hill of Versailles.
1631 Louis XIII commissions Philibert Le Roy to build a small palace on the site of the hunting pavilion. Work is completed in 1634.
1660 On the 7th June, the marriage of Louis XIV and Maria-Theresa, Infanta of Spain. They go to Versailles on 25th October.
1661 Death of the Prime Minister, Cardinal Mazarin, and beginning of Louis XIV's personal rule. Colbert is named Superintendent of Finances. Birth of the Grand Dauphin.
1663 The architect Le Vau builds the first Orangery and begins the Menagerie.
1664 In May, the King holds the festivities called *"Pleasures of the Enchanted Island"*.
1665 The first statues appear in the gardens.
The façades of the Marble Courtyard are adorned with busts. The Grotto of Tethys is begun.
1667 Digging begins on the Grand Canal.
1668 Adoption of Le Vau's project to enlarge the palace on the garden side by a "stone envelope".
On 18th July, Louis XIV holds the "Great Royal Entertainment" for his amazed courtiers.
1672 The Bathing Apartment on the ground-floor of the new palace is begun.
Work begins on the Ambassadors' Staircase.
1674 Year of the "great commission" of 24 statues for the gardens.
The last of the three great celebrations held by Louis XIV at Versailles.
1678 Jules Hardouin-Mansart designs plans for enlarging the palace. The garden terrace is removed to make room for the Hall of Mirrors.
1681 Completion of decoration of the State Apartments.
1682 On 6th May, Louis XIV decrees that Versailles is henceforth to be the official court residence and the seat of government.
1684 Completion of the Hall of Mirrors. Construction of the Orangery.
1685 Construction of the North Wing begins.
1687 Construction of the "Marble Trianon".
1689 In December, Louis XIV orders all the silverware and silver furniture of Versailles to be melted down.
1710 Completion of the Royal Chapel.
On 15th February, birth of the Duke of Anjou, (the future Louis XV), third son of the Duke of Burgundy.
1715 On 1st September, death of Louis XIV at 8.15 in the morning.
On 9th September, Louis XV leaves Versailles for Vincennes.
1722 On 15th June, Louis XV returns to make Versailles his residence.

1725 On 5th April, after breaking off her engagement to Louis XV, the Infanta, Doña Maria-Anna-Victoria, leaves Versailles for Spain.
1747 Marriage of the Dauphin to Maria-Josepha of Saxony.
1754 On 23rd August, birth of Louis-Auguste of France, the Duke of Berry (Louis XVI).
1770 On 16th May, marriage of the Dauphin to Marie-Antoinette of Lorraine, Archduchess of Austria. Opening of the Royal Opera built by Gabriel.
1771 Project for reconstructing all palace façades facing the town. The Louis XV Wing is begun by Gabriel.
1774 On 10th May, Louis XV dies of small-pox at Versailles.
1783 Signature of the Treaties which put an end to the war and confirm the independence of the United States of America. Construction begins on Marie-Antoinette's Hamlet at Trianon.
1789 On 5th May, opening of the States General in the *Salle des Menus Plaisirs*.
On 6th October, after the invasion of the palace, the Royal Family and the whole Court leave Versailles for Paris, never to return.
1792 On 20th October, following a proposition by the *député* Roland, the Convention orders the sale of the royal furniture.
1793 On 21st January, Louis XVI, condemned to death, is decapitated in Paris.
On 16th October, Marie-Antoinette is led to the scaffold.
1814 Louis XVIII orders all the palace apartments to be "restored to a habitable state".
1833 On 1st September, King Louis-Philippe orders the transformation of the palace of Versailles into a Museum of French History.
1837 On 10th June, inauguration of the Museum of Versailles.
1871 On 18th January, the German Empire is proclaimed in the Hall of Mirrors.
On 12th March, the National Assembly meets in the Opera.
1919 On 28th June 1919, the Allied Powers and Germany sign the Treaty of Versailles ending the first world war.
1957 Reopening of the entirely restored Royal Opera.
1962 General de Gaulle, President of the Republic, decides on the complete restoration of the Grand Trianon.
1975 Restoration of the Queen's Bedchamber.
1978 Reopening of the Consulate and Empire Rooms.
1980 Restoration of the furniture in the King's Bedchamber and the Hall of Mirrors.

▲

VERSAILLES
AND THE PASSING
OF TIME

« VERSAILLES »
THE CHATEAU AROUND 1668,
PAINTED BY PATEL

5

« *Versailles efface tous les palais enchantés de l'Histoire et de la Fable. C'est dans cette Maison royale et charmante que vous êtes invités à venir Peuples de la Terre, Curieux et Savants.* »

Originally a simple brick and stone château built by Louis XIII and later a gigantic palace in which Louis XIV wanted to embody the image of magnificence which characterized his reign, Versailles contains one and a half centuries of French art as it developed. The descendants of the *Great King* gradually transformed the interior of the château. Superb works of art were created in the private apartments and at Trianon. During the 18th century, however, they were irreparably damaged and time also destroyed some of the beauty of Versailles.

During the Revolution, the château was stripped of its furniture and, to create the Museum of French History in the 19th century, Louis-Philippe drastically altered a great number of apartments. The disappearance of their decoration is regrettable, particularly in the North and South Wings where famous residents, Princes of the Blood and high-ranking dignitaries once lived. Masterpieces of decorative art, witnesses to the refinement of the *Ancien Régime* and to the mastery of its artists, were sacrificed. The Chapel, Opera and Royal Apartments were, however, spared.

Dedicated "to all the glories of France", the Museum was inaugurated on 10th June 1837. Its reorganization, begun by Pierre de Nolhac at the beginning of this century, has been pursued with the attention to authentic detail demanded in our time. Through donations, the return of precious furnishings and a considerable amount of restoration work, the attraction of Versailles for visitors from all over the world, for history enthusiasts, art lovers or simply for sightseers, has been continually growing.

▲
VERSAILLES AND THE
MUSEUM OF
FRENCH HISTORY

◄ THE MAIN GATEWAY

THE COURTYARDS

The Great Courtyard is lined to the north and south by the Ministers' Wings. It was closed to the west, almost at the level of the equestrian statue of Louis XIV, by a second gilded railing. The Royal Courtyard lies between the Marble Courtyard and the King's statue. The buildings lining the Marble Courtyard correspond to the wings of Louis XIII's château. From here, the vast panorama stretches to the east far beyond the town.

THE QUEEN'S APARTMENT

8. Peace Drawing-Room
9. Queen's Bedchamber
10. Room of the Queen's Gentlemen
11. The *"Grand Couvert"* Antechamber
12. Guard Room
13. Queen's Staircase
14. Loggia

* THE QUEEN'S PRIVATE CABINETS

a. Bathchamber
b. Library Annexe
c. Gilded Cabinet
d. Gilded Library
e. The Meridian Cabinet
f. Duchess of Burgurdy's former Cabinet

* THE APARTMENT OF MADAME DE MAINTENON

g.-h. Antechambers
i. Bedchamber
j. State Cabinet

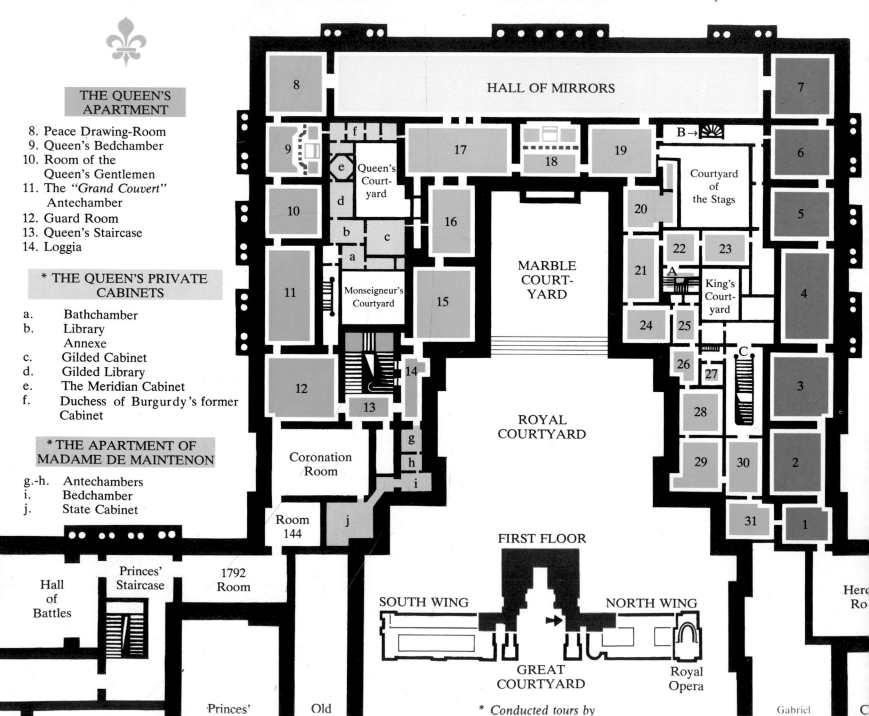

HALL OF MIRRORS

8 7

9 f B→

17 18 19 6

Queen's Courtyard Courtyard of the Stags 5

e

10 d 20

b c 16 22 23

a 21 A 4

11 King's Courtyard

Monseigneur's Courtyard 15 MARBLE COURT-YARD 24 25

26 C 3

12 14 27

13 28

g ROYAL COURTYARD 29 30 2

Coronation Room h

i 31 1

j

Room 144

FIRST FLOOR

Hall of Battles Princes' Staircase 1792 Room

SOUTH WING NORTH WING

Herº Roº

Princes' Courtyard Old Wing

GREAT COURTYARD Royal Opera

* *Conducted tours by National Museum guides*

Gabriel staircase

THE PALACE

THE STATE APARTMENT

1. Chamber of Abundance
2. Venus Room
3. Diana Room
4. Mars Room
5. Mercury Room
6. Apollo Room
7. War Drawing-Room

*THE KING'S APARTMENT

5. Guard Room
6. *"Grand Couvert"* Antechamber
7. Bull's-Eye Antechamber
8. King's Bedchamber
9. Council Chamber

*THE KING'S PRIVATE SUITE

0. Bedchamber
1. The Clock Cabinet
2. Antechamber of the Dogs
3. Dining-Room of the Cabinets
4. Private Cabinet
5. The Annexe or *Arrière-Cabinet*
6. Gilded Cabinet
7. Bathchamber
8. Louis XVI's Library
9. The Dining-Room of the New Rooms
0. Buffet Room
1. Louis XVI's Games Room
A. King's Stairway
B. Semicircular staircase
C. Louis-Philippe Staircase

Upper vestibule of the chapel	17th century Rooms
Royal Chapel	Smalah Courtyard

THE CHATEAU ▶
IN 1722
BY P.D. MARTIN

THE COURTYARDS
IN 1689
BY J.-B. MARTIN ▶

THE NORTH WING

AND THE 17TH CENTURY COLLECTIONS

The North Wing was chosen to display the 17th century paintings against a background of fabrics decorated with motifs of the time. The chronological order in which the paintings have been hung illustrates the reigns of Louis XIII and Louis XIV. Among the individual themes to which each room is dedicated are, on the ground-floor, the life of Louis XIII, the regency of Anne of Austria, the childhood of Louis XIV, the Jansenist movement and the Fronde, the first artists of Versailles and France's external policy at the beginning of Louis XIV's reign. The young King wanted to add to his military and diplomatic successes the prestige of a refined civilization and he had the good fortune to see a host of talented artists grow and work around him. The various stages in the building of Versailles are illustrated in paintings such as the one by Patel (see p. 4-5). In the last few rooms, life at Court is evoked with its receptions, banquets, the young sovereign's entourage and, finally, the interest in the development of the sciences.

On the first floor, two rooms are dedicated to various episodes in the wars fought by Louis XIV. The Court followed the army as it moved around. We are reminded of the King's passion for buildings by the views of the Royal Châteaux; then come por-

10

traits of the painters and sculptors who worked on their decoration. Louis XIV's close entourage, his ministers and the royal family are presented in the following rooms which contain several master-pieces by Mignard. After an evocation of the grave political decisions which cast a shadow over the end of his reign, the grace of the Princesses who charmed the Court brightens the last few rooms.

Finally, as a witness to the magnificence of the longest reign in the history of France, a cartoon for a tapestry calls to mind the predominance of France in 17th century Europe.

THE ROYAL CHAPEL

The chapel as it is today is the castle's fifth. Dedicated to Saint Louis, it is in the form of a Palatine chapel and consists of two storeys. A base of strong pillars supports the Corinthian colonnade on the upper storey. Above the aisles and ambulatory are wide galleries opening onto the central nave.

The royal gallery on the upper floor faces the altar by Van Clève which is surmounted by the beautiful organ-loft by Cliquot. The pillars are decorated with sculptures depicting the Old and New Testaments, the joint work of a large group of artists.

The gold and white harmony of the chapel, which was the setting for the religious ceremonies of the Court of France, is infused with warmth by the ceiling paintings.

In the archings and between the windows are painted prophets, evangelists and simulated architecture. Light pours directly onto the various scenes from the arched windows, thus enhancing the richness of the gold and the vivid colours.

The upper vestibule of the chapel links it with the State Apartments.

THE HERCULES ROOM

During the greater part of Louis XIV's reign, the Hercules Room of today served as the palace chapel.

All the walls are covered with marble of various hues from several regions of France. The fireplace of Antin marble is adorned with magnificent gilt bronzes carved by Antoine Vassé.

The ceiling was entrusted to François Lemoine who painted it from 1733 to 1736. Over one hundred figures represent the Apotheosis of Hercules, demonstrating that "Virtue raises man above himself, causes him to surmount the most difficult tasks and the greatest obstacles and leads him finally to immortality", as the painter wrote. The arrangement and colours were chosen by Lemoine to harmonize with the two great paintings by Veronese : *Christ's Meal in the Home of Simon the Pharisee* and *Elizier and Rebecca.* Louis XV was dazzled by the sight of this ceiling and named Lemoine Head Painter to the King, but the exhausted artist scarcely enjoyed his success as he committed suicide several months later.

THE
MAIN ALTAR AND
◀ THE ORGAN-LOFT

« MEAL AT THE HOUSE
OF SIMON »,
BY VERONESE ▶

THE STATE APARTMENT

This apartment, on the first floor of the château's central section, nothern side, was lived in by Louis XIV from 1673 to 1682. In that year, the King left it for a new apartment surrounding the Marble Courtyard. These rooms were set aside from then on for the famous Court receptions called "*Apartment*" evenings.

1 THE CHAMBER OF ABUNDANCE

When the chapel occupied the site of the Hercules Drawing-Room, this room served as a vestibule leading to the galleries and also opened onto the Cabinet of Curios and Rare Objects. The collections of gold and silver plate kept in the latter room inspired the decorative theme : abundance or "royal magnificence" as depicted in the gold monochrome overdoor, by René-Antoine Houasse, and on the ceiling. The walls are hung with green Genoan velvet trimmed with a gold galloon rewoven after 17th century designs. Portraits of princes belonging to Louis XIV's family are displayed in this room.

2 THE VENUS ROOM

Under Louis XIV, this and the following room opened onto the top of the famous Ambassadors' Staircase, demolished by Louis XV. The ceiling painting, the work of R.-A. Houasse, shows, in the centre, "Venus subjugating the Gods and Powers".

In the archings, historical scenes evoke events of Louis XIV's reign.

The back wall is lined with marble Ionic columns and pilasters. On the side walls, ingenious paintings of false perspectives lead the eye through a series of courtyards and galleries of ancient palaces. Between the windows, the artist, Jacques Rousseau, has even painted statues of Meleager and Atalanta which seem perfectly real.

Opposite the windows, between the two doors, a niche contains a real statue of the young Louis XIV, by Jean Warin. The King is represented in full length, dressed in ancient military costume.

On "*Apartment*" evenings, pyramids of fruit mingled with flowers were created on tables for the light meal held here.

14

3 THE DIANA ROOM

The central ceiling painting, by Gabriel Blanchard, depicts the legend of Diana and represents Apollo's sister, the Queen of the Night, presiding over hunting and navigation. These themes are illustrated in the archings by scenes taken from Antiquity, the work of Audran and Charles de Lafosse. In 1685, Louis XIV had his bust by Bernini placed in this room, where eight others were recently added to it. A billiard-table stood in the middle of the room.

Over the fireplace hangs a moving painting, "The Sacrifice of Iphigenia", by de Lafosse, and a painting by Blanchard, ''Diana and Endymion'', adorns the opposite wall.

4 THE MARS ROOM

Originally intended as the guard room, the Mars Room was later used for balls or games. On either side of the fireplace the musicians' galleries were set up. This room was once furnished with two large marquetry cabinets, seats covered in damask or velvet, like the walls, and two large mirrors which sparkled with the reflection of the chandeliers and candelabra.

War themes, the work of Audran, Jouvenet and Houasse, are painted on the ceiling. In the centre, Mars is riding in a wolf-drawn chariot. Above the fireplace hangs the well-known work by Domenichino, "David playing the Harp".

On the right hangs the painting by Le Brun "The Tent of Darius". On the side walls hang official portraits : Maria Leczinska by C. Van Loo and Louis XV by Rigaud.

THE
MERCURY
ROOM
▼

THE ▶
CEILING OF
THE APOLLO ROOM

5 THE MERCURY ROOM

The ceiling of this room is entirely the work of Jean-Baptiste de Champaigne (1631-1681). The central subject is "Mercury in a chariot drawn by two cocks, preceded by the Morning Star and accompanied by the Arts and Sciences".

This room first served as an antechamber, then as the State Bedchamber. The bed stood at the end of the room behind a silver balustrade. The rest of the furniture was also made of silver, but it was all melted down in 1689.

The automaton clock, made in 1706 by Morand for Louis XIV, has always stood here. Every hour, as the chimes sound the notes of an old melody, "the statue of Louis XIV comes out of the portico and a figure of Fame descends from a cloud".

6 THE APOLLO ROOM

This room, where the throne once stood, was designed as a magnificent, climactic end to the State Apartments. Under its ceiling dedicated to the sun god, the King would grant his state audiences to the ambassadors. The furniture here was sumptuous. On *"Apartment"* evenings, the Apollo Room was devoted to the joys of music and dancing. The ceiling is divided into five large compartments painted by a brilliant pupil of Le Brun, Charles de Lafosse, who was fascinated by colour and light. In the round central section held by eight gilt figures, the artist has portrayed "Apollo in his chariot drawn by four horses and accompanied by the Seasons"; below are two women symbolizing Royal Magnificence and France. The figures in the corners represent the four parts of the world.

Over the chimney is one of the portraits of Louis XIV in royal dress by Hyacinthe Rigaud. Another portrait of Louis XVI by Callet, also in royal dress, hangs opposite.

At the back of the room, a tapestry hangs where the throne once stood, below the bolts which held the canopy. The decoration is completed by guilded wood candlestands made for the Hall of Mirrors in 1770 at the occasion of the Dauphin's marriage to Marie-Antoinette.

There is also a rug commissioned from the Savonnerie tapestry works and a chandelier.

7 THE WAR DRAWING-ROOM

The marble-lined walls are adorned with gilt bronze war motifs. The ceiling represents France, and Victories and the allied powers are portrayed in the coves. Between the door to the Apollo Room and a false mirror door is the famous stucco relief, by Coysevox, of Louis XIV on horseback trampling on his enemies while Glory crowns him. The sculpture is held up by captives chained with flowers and surmounts a bas-relief of Clio writing the King's History.

THE
WAR
DRAWING-ROOM ▶

◄ PRECEDING PAGE:
THE HALL
OF MIRRORS

THE CEILING ►
OF THE PEACE
DRAWING-ROOM

THE HALL OF MIRRORS

The Hall of Mirrors, 243 feet long, is lit by seventeen high, arched windows on the first floor of the west façade of the palace. These are matched on the opposite wall by arcades adorned with French mirrors.

Like the War and Peace Drawing-Rooms, the Hall of Mirrors was built by Mansart and Le Brun from 1678 to 1686.

The Hall occupies the site of the terrace created by Le Vau between the King's and Queen's apartments. Between windows and arcades stand Rance marble pilasters on a white marble background. Above the gilt bronze, French Order capitals runs an entablature decorated with royal crowns and the order of Saint Michael. Gilt stucco trophies and weapons dominate the cornice. Louis XIV had some of the finest antiques in his collection placed in the niches between the pilasters.

The Hall of Mirrors served as a passage for the royal family on its way to the chapel. It was here, too, that celebrations or state receptions were held in honour of princely marriages or of an extraordinary embassy. The treaty ending the 1914-1918 war was signed here on 28th June 1919.

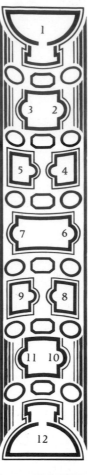

Themes of the nine large paintings on the ceiling from the War Drawing-Room to the Peace Drawing-Room :

1 — *Alliance of Germany and Spain with Holland* — 1672
▼ 2 — *Crossing the Rhine in the presence of the enemy* — 1672
▼ 3 — *The King takes Maestricht in thirteen days* — 1673
4 — *The King giving orders to attack four of Holland's strongholds at the same time* — 1672
5 — *The King arming his fleet and his army* — 1672
6 — *The King governs alone* — 1661
7 — *Pomp of France's neighbouring powers.*
8 — *Franche-Comté conquered a second time* - 1674
9 — *Resolution passed to make war on the Dutch* — 1671
10 — *Capture of the city and citadel of Ghent in six days* — 1678
11 *Spanish action destroyed by the capture of Ghent.*
12 — *Holland accepts peace and breaks with Germany and Spain* — 1678

THE QUEEN'S APARTMENT

8 THE PEACE DRAWING-ROOM

Like the War Drawing-Room, the Peace Drawing-Room is a continuation of the Hall of Mirrors. The talent of Le Brun has expressed itself here in the marble panels, the bronze trophies, the mirrors sparkling in the abundant light and in the painted and gilded ceiling. In contrast to the severly dramatic themes of the War Drawing-Room, the images here are peaceful ones. The ceiling portrays the Apotheosis of France and above the large, green marble fireplace hangs an oval painting by Lemoine, "Louis XV bestowing peace on Europe", dated 1729.

◄ DETAIL OF
THE CEILING IN
THE HALL OF MIRRORS

▲
THE
PEACE
DRAWING-ROOM

MARIE-ANTOINETTE AND
HER CHILDREN
(DETAIL)

THE
QUEEN'S
CHAMBER ▶

▼

9 THE QUEEN'S CHAMBER

This room was decorated from 1671 to 1680 for Maria-Theresa and renovated in 1729 for Maria Leczinska. The ceiling contains four grisaille medallions by Boucher representing Charity, Abundance, Fidelity and Prudence. The overdoors were painted by Natoire and de Troy in 1734. In 1770, Marie-Antoinette had the two-headed eagle of the House of Austria added to the corners of the ceiling and, in 1773, she ordered the Savonnerie tapestry portraits of her mother, her brother and Louis XVI, her husband, to be set over the mirrors between the windows, above the fireplace and opposite it.

When it was decided to reconstitute the whole décor of this room, which had been stripped bare, Marie-Antoinette's last "summer wall-hanging", delivered in 1787 by Desfarges of Lyons, was chosen. It is of "white Tours silk embroidered with bouquets of flowers entwined around peacocks' tails". The jewelry-cabinet by Schwerdfeger, adorned with miniatures and Sèvres porcelain figures, stands once more on the left of the bed, which has had its gilded balustrade remade. The fireplace again has its screen by Sené as well as the andirons chosen by Marie-Antoinette. Finally, two armchairs and eight folding-stools complete the ensemble.

10 THE ROOM OF THE QUEEN'S GENTLEMEN

It was here that the Queen held her "circles" and granted her state audiences. All that remains of the décor created for Queen Maria-Theresa is the ceiling painted in 1671 by Michel Corneille on the theme of famous women of Antiquity practising the arts and sciences.

In 1785, the marble and stucco-work on the walls were replaced by waist-high wainscoting, several mirrors and an apple-green wall-hanging gallooned with gold. A very fine fireplace of slate-blue marble ornamented with bronzes by Gouthière was placed here. Several years ago, the décor of this room was entirely reconstituted as it was in Marie-Antoinette's time. Two chests-of-drawers and two corner cupboards executed by Riesener in 1786 have been returned to their intended positions along the walls. A large tapestry portrait of Louis XV, a Louis XVI fire-screen, a set of folding-stools, a late 18th century chandelier and a magnificent Savonnerie carpet complete the décor.

In this room, the Queen held her audiences and had the ladies recently admitted to Court presented to her.

11 THE "GRAND COUVERT" DINING-ROOM

The décor created for Queen Maria-Theresa has remained partly intact. The lower part of the walls is lined with marble panels. The war themes on the ceiling are a reminder that this room was originally a guard-room. In the corners of the ceiling are large gilded trophies surmounted by cupids. The central ceiling painting, by Claude Vignon, has disappeared and been replaced with an old replica of « Darius Tent », by Le Brun.

This antechamber was once used for theatrical performances, balls or concerts. Finally, it came to be used for the "grand couvert" when the King, in the company of the Queen, dined here in public.

The large Languedoc marble fireplace which once stood against the wall of the Room of the Queen's Gentlemen and the doors in the north wall were replaced in recent years and this room has now been chosen to display the famous painting by Madame Vigée-Lebrun, "Marie-Antoinette and her children".

12 THE ROOM
OF THE QUEEN'S GUARD

The décor comes from the former Jupiter Drawing-Room, the King's first State Cabinet. On the site of this room once stood the galleries of a chapel destroyed in 1676. A floor was laid and walls lined with green and red marble panels edged with black marble mouldings. The six gilt metal bas-reliefs above the doors are by the sculptors Le Gros and Massou. Noël Coypel carried out the whole painted decoration. In an octagonal painting in the centre of the ceiling, the ruler of the gods is represented crossing the sky in a silver chariot drawn by eagles, accompanied by allegories of Justice and Piety, which are also portrayed in the archings by examples drawn from Antiquity. Two paintings form part of the mural decoration, above the fireplace, "A Sacrifice to Jupiter", and opposite, "The Dance of the Corybants".

In this room, the Queen's guard stood watch night and day. Their devotion enabled Marie-Antoinette to escape the fury of the crowd which invaded the palace on the 6th October 1789.

THE CORONATION ROOM

The former "great guard room" was chosen by Louis-Philippe, when the Museum of French History was created, to evoke the pomp and splendour of the Empire by its decoration and the display of three canvases of immense proportions, the "Coronation of Josephine", the "Distribution of the Eagle Standards", a masterly work by David, and the "Battle of Aboukir" by Gros, commissioned by Murat.

THE HALL OF BATTLES

The Hall of Battles is Louis-Philippe's most important creation at Versailles; 30 huge paintings, 82 busts of warriors and 16 bronze plaques on which are engraved the names of heroes who died for France form an imposing summary of the history of France from the battle of Tolbiac, won by Clovis in 496, to Napoleon's victory at Wagram in 1809.

The Queen's Staircase (13) was built between 1679 and 1681 and extended by the addition of a loggia in 1701. Multi-coloured marble forms the basis of its decoration both for the slabs and balustrade of the staircase and on the wall panels. The overdoors are adorned with bas-reliefs of young children and sphinxes of "gilt-metal" like the trophy in the niche on the landing representing two genii bearing the royal monogram surmounted by two doves. The large trompe-l'œil painting opposite the loggia extends the sense of space of this superb stairway which leads to the Queen's Apartment. It also led to the King's Apartment from 1682 when Louis XIV had it moved to the section surrounding the Marble Courtyard.

MADAME DE MAINTENON'S APARTMENT

This apartment, where Madame de Maintenon lived from 1682 to 1715, follows on from the King's Apartment and is reached via the loggia of the Queen's Staircase.

The two antechambers contain 16th century portraits from the Roger de Gaignières collection.

The bedchamber was reduced in size in the 19th century as an unfortunate result of the building of the Stucco Staircase; in the remaining space are displayed gouaches by Jean Cotelle depicting the gardens of Versailles.

Portraits of the princesses and ladies of Louis XIV's family hang in the State Cabinet. In this Cabinet, hung with crimson brocade, Madame de Maintenon often received the Royal Family and the young ladies of the Institute of Saint-Cyr would come here to act in Racine's tragedies.

THE QUEEN'S PRIVATE CABINETS

Situated behind the Queen's Apartment and opening onto rather dark courtyards, the Private Cabinets bore witness to each sovereign's desire for privacy. They consist principally of a bathchamber and its retiring room, two libraries, a drawing-room and a cabinet called the Meridian Cabinet. Created at the time of Louis XIV for Maria-Theresa, they were lived in for many years by Maria-Leczinska. There, she found the place she needed to talk, embroider or paint and she had the rooms adorned with rococo wainscoting which has since gone. The Drawing-Room or Gilded Cabinet was entirely redecorated in 1783 in the antique style. The wood-panelling is decorated with sphinxes and an incense-burner on a tripod. Created by Marie-Antoinette's architect, Mique, it was carved by the Rousseau brothers, who also decorated the Meridian Cabinet. After crossing the library which was once Maria-Theresa's oratory and later Maria Leczinska's art studio, one enters a small octagonal drawing-room, one of the most charming in Versailles and named after the Queen's habit of resting there in the middle of the day.

The ornamentation of the Meridian Cabinet dates back to 1781. It symbolizes marital love and is an allusion to the birth of the Dauphin.
►

THE ALCOVE ▶
IN THE KING'S
BEDCHAMBER

THE KING'S APARTMENT

The Queen's Staircase gives access to this apartment. The first two rooms, the Guard Room and the "Grand Couvert" Antechamber (15-16) are decorated with battle scenes by Parrocel.

17 THE BULL'S-EYE ROOM

Until 1701 there were two rooms here. When Louis XIV made the adjoining room his chamber, this room was created out of the former two and a large bull's-eye window placed in the raised ceiling. Around it, two teams of sculptors carved the remarkable cornice depicting "Children's Games". A large canvas by Nocret shows Louis XIV and his family as gods of Antiquity. This was the Antechamber where the courtiers who were "allowed to attend the King's rising ceremony" waited to be shown into the Bedchamber.

18 THE KING'S BEDCHAMBER

It was only in 1701 that Louis XIV decided to make this his chamber. Previously it had been the State Drawing-Room of the small Louis XIII château, which was lit by the windows overlooking the courtyard and gardens, as the Hall of Mirrors did not exist before 1678. The removal of the windows on the garden side entailed the renewal of the décor in 1679. Then, in 1701, an alcove was set into the wall, its upper section adorned with a gilded carving, by Nicolas Coustou, of "France watching over the King in his slumber". Taupin, Goupil, Bellan and Dugoulon carved the youthful figures and garlands of flowers framing the portraits over the doors. These depict "Saint Magdalen" by Domenichino, a self-portrait by Van Dyck, "Saint John the Baptist", attributed to Caraciolo and "François d'Aytona" by Van Dyck. Each morning and evening, the room would be filled with life as the lords entered for the King's "Rising" and "Retiring" ceremonies. Both Louis XV and Louis XVI, who had bedchambers in the Private Apartment, continued to observe the ritual instituted by Louis XIV. The furniture was extremely sumptuous and brocade and velvet wall-hangings alternated according to the seasons.

▲
THE
BULL'S EYE
ROOM

LOUIS XIV ▶
IN HIS BEDCHAMBER,
BY MAROT

28

Restoration of the King's Chamber was completed in 1980. A brocade of great richness was rewoven after fragments of a summer wallhanging which was still in existence. This fabric covers the alcove wall and doors, the bed and seats. The windows are hung with crimson silk curtains. The wainscoting, shutters and balustrade were removed, repaired and gilded once more. The paintings of biblical themes, by Valentin de Boulogne and Lanfranco, were returned to the attic were they had hung previously. This restoration, made possible by the generosity of donors and the State and the efforts of contemporary artists, has recreated in all its magnificence this sanctuary of the monarchy of divine right.

19 THE COUNCIL CHAMBER

In 1755, Louis XV commissioned Gabriel to link the King's State Cabinet overlooking the Marble Court-yard to the Cabinet of Terms which opened onto the Hall of Mirrors. To the remaining sections of the former décor the architect added wood-panels carved by J.-A. Rousseau depicting the King's various *councils*: peace, war and the navy. A council table, covered with the same brocaded satin as the curtains, is a reminder of this room's rôle during the *Ancien Régime*. On the red marble fireplace stands a gilt-bronze clock made for Louis XV as well as two Sèvres porcelain vases with chased bronzes by Thomire.

THE KING'S PRIVATE CABINETS

A series of rooms parallel to the State Apartment continues the King's Apartment on the first floor of the château (plans n° 20 to 31).

Louis XIV reserved these rooms for collections of paintings and rare objects. From 1738 on, Louis XV had Gabriel make this collector's apartment into one suitable to live in.

The first room was bedchamber of Louis XV and Louis XVI. It still has its wainscoting by Verberckt and its fine Serancolin marble fireplace, but its rich furniture has gone. To give a little life to this room, the alcove is to be hung in a brocade tapestry like the model delivered in 1785. On the left is the dressing-room.

The famous astronomical clock, after which the room is still named the Clock Cabinet, was installed in 1760 on a marble base in front of a large mirror. Designed by Passement, with a mechanism by Dauthiau, it was adorned with gilt bronze by Caffiéri. It still indicates the hour, month, date and the phase of the moon. In the crystal globe at the top, the planets revolve around the sun according to the Copernican system.

The Clock Cabinet leads, on the left, to the

Antechamber of the Dogs and the After-Hunt Dining-Room. To the right it leads to the King's Private Cabinet, given its final appearance in 1760. Louis XV made this one of the most beautiful rooms in the château. In 1738 the Italian griotte marble fireplace was installed. To the medal-chest delivered by Gaudreaux in 1739 were added, in 1755, Joubert's corner cupboards, set against Verberckt's masterly wainscoting, and later, the famous roll-top writing-desk, commissioned from Oeben in 1760 and completed by Riesener in 1769. Thomire's bronzes and the chairs by

Foliot, covered in a red damask also used for the curtains, restore its regal luxury to this important room. Beyond the Annexe, on the site of the Small Gallery decorated by Mignard and destroyed in 1752, are the New Rooms which include Madame Adélaïde's Gilded Cabinet with its fine wainscoting by Verberckt, Louis XVI's Library, given an intimate charm by the recently restored fabrics of painted Pekin silk, and the Porcelain Cabinet. Further on, Louis XVI's Games Room, formerly Louis XIV's Cabinet of Curios, opens onto the Billiards Room.

THE
KING'S PRIVATE
◀ CABINET

▲
MADAME
ADELAIDE'S
MUSIC ROOM

35

THE KING'S PRIVATE APARTMENTS

Located on different levels of the roofing over the King's Apartments and overlooking the entrance courtyards to the château and the Courtyard of the Stags, this was Louis XV's private realm, inaccessible to his courtiers, where he would come to live in simplicity surrounded by those close to him. The rooms, often small in size, are filled with unexpected charm. The talented decorators managed to hide their rather thankless proportions by the harmonious arrangement of the wood-panelling. In Madame du Barry's Apartment, deep window recesses elegantly disguise the sloping roof.

The purpose, shape and decoration of the numerous rooms in these private apartments were altered many times. They were used as recreation rooms, pantries and workshops. Since they communicated so easily with the King's Private Cabinets, Louis XV decided to create an apartment there for his favourite Madame du Barry.

In the rooms occupied by the Countess until the King's death in 1774, skilful restoration work has brought back the refined hall-mark of the 18th century. The well-stocked shelves of the library, a settee in the alcove, a small desk, a chair and, in front of the window, a parrot-cage embellished with Dresden china flowers, restore its intimate charm to this tiny room. The row of rooms overlooking the Marble Courtyard was once magnificently furnished. Their multicoloured decoration was removed in 1767 when the wainscoting was gilded for Madame du Barry. The former furnishings, now scattered, were replaced by furniture of rare quality, such as the Furniture of the Gods in the State Cabinet, which gave a new splendour to these once so luxurious rooms. The freshness of colour of the Martin varnish has been restored to the dining-room, antechamber and bathroom. Their decoration is once again as Louis XV and his mistress knew it.

It is possible to visit Madame du Barry's apartment only if guided by an official National Museums lecturer. This is also true for Madame de Pompadour's apartment above the State Apartment.

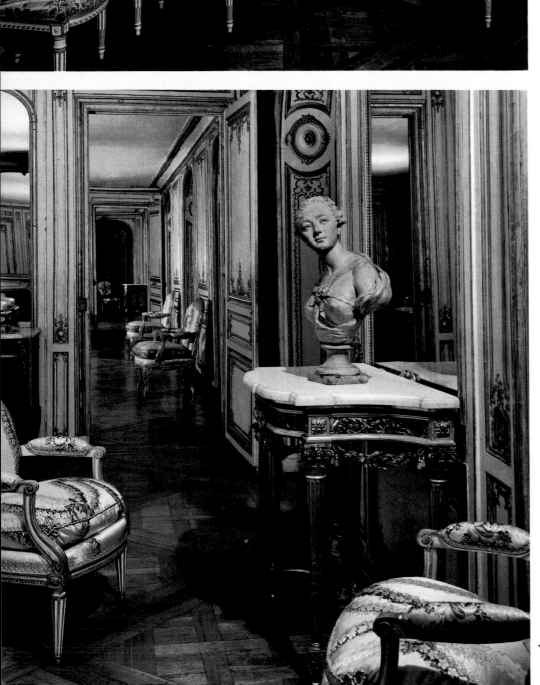

VIEW FROM
THE BEDCHAMBER TO
◄ MADAME DU BARRY'S CABINET

THE PASTORAL
CONCERT,
PAINTED BY DROUAIS ►

THE GROUND-FLOOR OF THE MAIN BUILDING

AND THE 18TH CENTURY COLLECTIONS

Under the *Ancien Régime*, this part of the château, disfigured by Louis-Philippe, contained several of the finest apartments in Versailles. Since the museum's reorganization, this section has contained the 18th century collections.

Paintings depicting the Regency and the beginning of Louis XV's reign are displayed in the Dauphine's Apartment. Scarcely any of Gabriel's superb decoration remains. Only the Private Cabinet now has its former freshness, after delicate restoration work.

In the Dauphin's Apartment the original decoration has been restored to the library, with its wood-panelling painted in blue and yellow Martin lacquer, and to the bedroom, where the fireplace with its chased bronze by Caffiéri is surmounted by pier-glasses adorned with carving by Verbeckt. In the Corner Cabinet between these two rooms hang portraits of women which show Nattier's skill in capturing the youthful grace of the Princesses, his favourite models.

At the time of Louis XIV, the Lower Gallery, in the middle of the château, gave one direct access from the Marble Courtyard to the Water Parterre. Later, to accomodate Louis XV's daughters, it was divided up into several apartments. Beyond lies a suite of rooms which were decorated with particular brilliance. Louis XIV's Bathing Apartment was panelled with marble and embellished with gilt bronze, paintings and superb wall-hangings. In the Octagonal Drawing-Room, twelve large statues form a zodiac. Hardly anything of this splendour remained after a number of apartments were created here for Madame Adélaïde, Madame Victoire and Madame de Pompadour. These suites, disfigured by Louis-Philippe, are being restored to their 18th century state.

The walls of the drawing-room of the Ambassadors' Staircase, one of the wonders of Louis XIV's Versailles and destroyed in 1752, are now as they were originally. In the rooms surrounding the Marble Courtyard, where the Queen had her private suite, the décors from the reign of Louis XVI and Marie-Antoinette have been recreated.

THE
DAUPHIN'S
◀ LIBRARY

THE DAUPHIN'S
BEDCHAMBER
BEFORE 1980 ▶

THE ROYAL OPERA

The wars at the end of Louis XIV's reign prevented the execution of Mansart's project for the creation of a ballet room in the north wing.

Under Louis XV, Gabriel presented new plans for the same site in 1748. After a long interruption due to lack of money, work was resumed by Gabriel in 1768 in anticipation of the Dauphin's marriage to Archduchess Marie-Antoinette, and completed in spring, 1770.

The room has an almost oval shape, and its entire décor is of gilded wood or simulated marble : columns, balconies, balustrades and panels. Wood was chosen because of the excellent acoustics that can be created. Gabriel entrusted the painter Durameau with the task of « deciding all the shades and blends needed to create an overall harmony and a beautiful finish ». It is to the same artist that we owe the twelve painted ceilings of the colonnade depicting the « Loves of the Gods » and, above all, the large oval painting which forms the ceiling and portrays « Apollo making crowns for illustrious men of the Arts ». All the decorative sculpture comes from Pajou's workshop : the bas-reliefs on the balconies (the Gods of Olympus on the first, children and the signs of the zodiac on the second), the scroll with the King's Arms held by two radiating figures of glory (above the stage), the groups of children, and the sphinxes and swans in the four proscenium lunettes, as well as its large trophies. Opposite the stage on the second floor, behind a sliding trellis, is the royal box, flanked by those of the ministers and the superintendent of buildings.

The overall colour-scheme is blue, set off with pink and gold. The seats and balustrades are covered in various kinds of velvet : almond-green and a closely-woven Utrecht blue. The sky-blue silks are magnificently embroidered in gold (on the curtain, the Arms of France alone contain nearly twenty pounds of gold !). In addition to the paintings, gilded carvings and embroidered silks, the crystal chandeliers and the mirrors in the colonnade heighten the sense of refinement of the decoration and create a magical atmosphere.

Restoration work completed in 1957 has once again endowed Versailles with the most sumptuous of Court theatres.

"SKY-BLUE, PINK AND GOLD"
THE MAGICAL DECORATION
OF THE OPERA ▶

THE CONSULATE
AND EMPIRE ROOMS

This section of the Museum of French History is located in the attic storey and ground-floor of the South Wing with an extension above the Queen's Apartment.

It consists in part of paintings commissioned by Napoleon I for the imperial residences. Before taking the "stucco staircase", which leads to the "southern attics", the visitor has to go through one of the most popular creations in the Museum, the Coronation Room, named after the famous painting by David (sent to the Louvre in 1889 and replaced by a copy).

In these attics, against a background of fabrics woven from designs created to decorate the imperial palaces, hang the gouaches and small and medium format paintings which retrace the Napoleonic epic.

Through the gouaches by Bagetti one can follow step by step the entry of the French troops into Northern Italy during the First Italian Campaign. The painter Gros has commemorated, in a celebrated work, General Bonaparte's act of bravura on the bridge

at Arcole. Then follow the Egyptian expedition and the Battle of the Pyramids in July 1798, painted by Lejeune. Two of the most striking events of the Second Italian Campaign were the crossing of the Great Saint Bernard Pass by the French army in May 1800 and the victory at Marengo.

François Gérard, a pupil of David, became the fashionable portrait painter of the time, ''the king of painters and the painter of kings''. Versailles prides itself on its impressive set of miniature portraits known as Gérard's ''sketches.'' In a room dedicated to the Imperial Family gathered around the portrait of Napoleon (by Gérard) one may dream of the luxury of that new Court.

Paintings and watercolours trace the Third Coalition in 1805, against which the Emperor won the battle of Austerlitz on 2nd December.

Intellectual life is portrayed by the most impressive figures of this period.

A series of canvases is dedicated to the arrival of Marie-Louise, the future Empress, and to the marriage celebrations in 1810.

After the cruel Spanish war and the march of the Great Army which occupied Moscow in 1812, the fierce resistance met with, as well as the terrible Russian winter, led to a reversal of the situation at the expense of the French.

In 1813, almost all of Europe joined forces against Napoleon. The last paintings depict the death throes of that grandiose epic which ended with the Hundred Days on the plains of Waterloo in June 1815 and the final exile to Saint Helena.

Under the *Ancien Régime*, the ground-floor of the South Wing, which is reached via the lower vestibule of the Princes' Staircase, contained some of the finest apartments in the château.

The rooms created by Louis-Philippe were reserved for the display of the large format paintings several of which are well-known, like « The Capitulation of Madrid », by Gros, or « The Cairo Uprising », a manifesto of pre-romantic art, by Girodet.

THE CORONATION
OF JOSEPHINE,
◀ BY DAVID

THE CAIRO
UPRISING,
BY GIRODET ▶

A GUIDE TO THE GARDENS AND THE GROVES

THE GREAT FOUNTAINS

Over one million gallons of water are required for the fountains of Versailles to play for one hour. Until recently, the water was drawn from nearby pools and the Seine by a gigantic pump at Marly, built between 1675 and 1683.

The great fountains are one of the most beautiful sights Versailles can offer. The sculptures adorning the pools were designed as part of the water display from which they derive their vitality and some of their extraordinary beauty.

Versailles is the place of triumph for
the gardens "à la française" with their
rigorously ordered parterres where
nature has been completely subjugated
by an architect-gardener. Le Nôtre
gave majestic dimensions to the main
axes already laid out under Louis XIII;
he created the magnificent expanses of
water in which the sky, foliage and
statues are reflected. Mansart shaped
the groves of Louis XIV's time into
architectural forms. The sketches for
the majority of the statues, vases and
fountains were the work of Le Brun.
Some of the groves have gone but,
three centuries after their creation, the
gardens of Versailles, inhabited by gods
of marble and bronze, continue to
attract crowds who have come there to
wander at leisure.

1 THE SOUTH PARTERRE

The South Parterre is reached by a
staircase flanked by cupids seated on
sphinxes, by Lerambert and Sarrazin.
Symmetrically placed on either side of
a central pathway, scrolls of box-tree
and flower-beds surround plain circular pools. The only embellishment of
this parterre is its floral decoration, and
each year, during the warm season, it
blossoms out in the traditional splendour which has earned it the name of
the Parterre of Flowers. Above it are
marble copings bearing bronze vases
filled in summer with pink or red
geraniums.

2 THE ORANGERY

This colossal building, constructed
from 1684 to 1686 by Jules Hardouin-
Mansart below the South Parterre,
consists of a central vaulted gallery,
516 feet long, lit by large arched
windows and extended by two lateral
galleries, each 372 feet long, which end
beneath the staircase of the Hundred
Steps. During the cold season the
galleries once contained thousands of
orange-trees, oleanders, pomegranates
or palm-trees. On fine days their exotic
vegetation is displayed for the admira-
tion of those strolling along the vast
avenues of the Orangery Parterre.
Beyond stretches the "lake" of the
Swiss Guards, created in 1679.

BRONZE VASES
WITH GERANIUMS,
◀ SOUTH PARTERRE

◄ THE PALACE
AND THE
ORANGERY

◄ ORANGERY
AND THE
LAKE OF
THE SWISS
GUARDS

49

3 THE WATER PARTERRE

This parterre, in front of the western façade of the palace, was laid out in 1684 on the initiative of Mansart. It consists of two rectangular stretches of water surrounded by a marble rim along which are placed sixteen bronze statues representing the rivers of France, nymphs and groups of children.

Cast by the Keller brothers, these statues are the work of the greatest sculptors of the 17th century : Coysevox, Tuby, Regnaudin, Le Hongre and Magnier.

The three projecting parts of the façade hold statues representing the twelve months of the year framing Apollo and Diana. On four pedestals before the façade stand four bronze statues after classical models : *Bacchus, Apollo, Mercury and Silenus.*

In the corners of the terrace are two splendid vases of carved marble; on the left, the War Vase, by Coysevox, and, on the right, the Peace Vase, by Tuby.

The two Fountains of the Animals, which flank the stairs leading to the Latona parterre, are an integral part of this unique ensemble, the water parterre.

4 THE FOUNTAIN AND PARTERRE OF LATONA

The parterre of Latona is in the shape of a horseshoe formed by stone copings surrounding two flower-beds separated by a wide central avenue. The flower-beds are lined with marble vases and the copings with statues, most of which are copies of antiques.

The parterre has three fountains, that of Latona and two Lizard Fountains. The main pool consists of three concentric marble bases surmounted by a white marble group, by Gaspard and Balthazar Marsy, representing Latona with her two children, Diana and Apollo, at her feet, imploring Jupiter to avenge her against the Lycian peasants who scorned her and were turned into frogs by the ruler of Olympus.

The Lizard Fountains, placed symmetrically in the centre of the two parterres of lawn and flowers forming the horseshoe, also portray the metamorphosis of the Lycian peasants.

THE PARTERRE
OF LATONA AND
◄ THE GREAT EAST-WEST AXIS

THE
GARDENS
OF VERSAILLES

51

5 THE SOUTH QUINCUNX

Like the North Quincunx, it is adorned with eight marble terms, carved in Rome after sketches by Poussin and bought by Louis XIV in 1683.

6 THE ROCKWORK GROVE

It was created between 1681 and 1683. Near the entrances are steps for the spectators to sit on. Opposite, is an admirable "rockwork cascade" of Madagascan shells.

7 THE QUEEN'S GROVE

We should notice the fine bronze Medici Venus, four busts on marble stands, a bronze replica of the "fighting gladiator" and a polychrome marble statue of Minerva.

8 THE FOUNTAIN OF AUTUMN

The octagonal pool contains a gilded lead group, representing Bacchus seated, fashioned by the Marsy brothers from sketches by Le Brun.

9 THE HALF-MOON AND KING'S GARDEN

The Half-Moon, or Mirror Pool, was formerly at the end of a vast artificial lake called the Royal Island, which Louis XVIII had replaced by an English garden.

10 THE FOUNTAIN OF WINTER

The centre of this round pool is decorated with a lead group by Girardon, executed from a sketch by Le Brun and representing Saturn, or Winter.

11 THE HALL OF CHESTNUT-TREES

This grove received its present appearance in 1704 when it was adorned with eight marble busts and two statues of which only one remains.

12 THE COLONNADE

This marble peristyle, 102 feet in diameter and adorned with thirty-two marble columns and as many pilasters, was built by Lapierre from sketches by Mansart. The numerous sculptures decorating the Colonnade are the work of a whole team, Coysevox, Mazière, Granier, Le Hongre, Le Conte and Tuby. The triangular tympani depict genii and cupid musicians, while heads of nymphs, naiads and forest deities adorn the keystones of the arches. The colonnade served as the setting for suppers and light meals held by day or by night.

13 THE GREEN CARPET OR ROYAL AVENUE

Already outlined under Louis XIII, the avenue was given its final shape by Le Nôtre: 70 yards wide and 366 yards long. It forms the largest part of the east-west axis. Its wide lawn is lined with two paths along which stand twelve statues and as many vases of white marble, the majority carved by students of the Academy of France in Rome.

The Green Carpet slopes down to the Chariot of Apollo. Each side of the Half-Moon, which lies between them, is adorned with a marble group, four terms and a classical statue.

14 THE FOUNTAIN OF APOLLO AND THE GRAND CANAL

The gilded lead group in the centre of an octagonal pool represents Apollo in his chariot, harnessed to four horses surrounded by monsters and tritons rising from the water to bring light to the earth. Tuby was inspired by an Italian painting in creating this powerful work, constructed horizontally to avoid breaking the long view of the Green Carpet and the Grand Canal.

The latter is in the shape of a cross with a short north arm leading to the Grand Trianon.

15 THE GROVE OF THE DOMES

In 1677, Mansart built two small white marble pavilions. The statues from the Grotto of Tethys, which had recently been destroyed, were placed in three latticework niches in 1684. At the same time, the two balustrades were reconstructed and adorned with bas-reliefs depicting *the arms of various nations.*

Though only the sites of these domed pavilions remain, most of the classical statues on pedestals ornamented with shells and icicles still exist.

16 THE FOUNTAIN OF ENCELADUS

It is named after the giant, (carved by G. Marsy in 1676), whom we see crushed by the mass of rocks fallen from the slopes of Mount Olympus. The spray coming from the titan's mouth is particularly strong and rises to a height of 75 feet.

17 THE OBELISK FOUNTAIN

It was built by Mansart in 1706. In the centre of the upper bowl is a clump of reeds from which gush nearly 230 sprays forming a cone.

18 THE FOUNTAIN OF SPRING

The round pool is adorned in the centre with a lead group by Tuby, representing Flora surrounded by flowers and cupids.

19 THE NORTHERN QUINCUNX

The Quincunx is on the right as one walks up the Avenue of the Seasons. It was formerly the Dauphin's grove and is adorned with several marble terms.

THE STAR GROVE

was once called the Mountain of Water and its pool, which contained many fountains, was removed in 1704. The grove consists of five paths forming a star.

20 THE FOUNTAIN OF SUMMER

This octagonal pool is adorned with a lead group representing Ceres, by Regnaudin. We turn left and go north into the grand avenue.

21 THE CHILDREN'S ISLAND

In the centre of the pool is a rock on which six children play and laugh while two little cupids splash about in the water. These figures, so full of gaiety, were carved by Hardy. The Green Ring lies to the east of the preceding pool. It is a simple grassy bowl surrounded by trees and was created in the 18th century.

22 THE BATHS OF APOLLO

In 1778, two years after the park was replanted, the painter Hubert Robert was entrusted with the creation of the new grove. He imagined an Anglo-chinese garden adorned with a small lake whose east bank would be lined with a huge artificial rock with grottos cut into it and decorated with columns.

The central grotto contains the famous group depicting Apollo waited on by Nymphs, by Girardon and Regnaudin. Lower down stand the Sun Horses, the one on the left by Marsy, the other by Guérin.

23 THE NORTH PARTERRE

From here we can admire at leizure the façade of the State Apartments overlooking the park, and, at right angles, the north wing of the palace, built by J. H.-Mansart. The entrance stairway is flanked by two copies of classical statues cast in bronze : the *Knife-grinder,* by Foggini, and the *Modest Venus,* by Coysevox. Along the paths lining this parterre to the north and west, stand a series of statues and terms. The central avenue leads beyond the Crown Fountains to one of the most graceful fountains in the Park of Versailles, the Pyramid Fountain, by Girardon.

Close to the Pyramid, at the entrance to the Water Avenue, lie the famous Baths of the Nymphs, a rectangular pool into which the water falls in a cascade.

THE FOUNTAIN
OF NEPTUNE
◀ IN 1700

24 THE WATER AVENUE OR AVENUE OF THE MARMOSETS

Its principal theme is child-hood. In each round, white marble pool are three children holding a pink marble bowl. The first fourteen groups, standing opposite each other on either side of the avenue, were placed here in 1670. The ensemble was later completed by eight more groups ornamenting the half-moon at the end of the Water Avenue.

25 THE DRAGON FOUNTAIN

This large circular pool is almost 130 feet in diameter. It is adorned with children riding dolphins and swans who seem to be fighting a furious dragon.

26 THE FOUNTAIN OF NEPTUNE

In 1678, le Nôtre planned the creation of the semicircular pool, which was completed only in 1741, under Louis XV.

It was L.-S. Adam who executed the central group of Neptune and Amphitrite. On the left, also in lead, Bouchardon fashioned the figure of Proteus mounted on a sea unicorn. On the right, the ocean god leaning on a conch held by fish is the work of Lemoine. At the end of the pool are two giant dragons mounted by two cupids by Bouchardon. This pool, as we see it today, was inaugurated by Louis XV who could then admire the ninety-nine magnificent jets of water which are the glory of this ensemble.

MARMOSETS
FROM THE
WATER AVENUE ▶

TRIANON

PLAN OF THE ENTRANCES :

1 - ROYAL PARADE-GROUND
2 - THE PALACE
3 - THE GREEN CARPET
4 - APOLLO'S CHARIOT
5 - THE GRAND TRIANON
6 - THE SMALL TRIANON AND MARIE-ANTOINETTE'S HAMLET

THE ▶
MAIN
GATEWAY

THE LEFT
WING ▶
AND
THE UPPER
GARDEN ▶

THE GRAND TRIANON

This is a palace in the Italian style, a single-storeyed building with a flat roof and a colonnade, built by Jules Hardouin-Mansart in 1687 to replace the smaller "Porcelain Trianon". All the rooms have high arched windows looking onto the garden or the Great Courtyard. The exterior décor consists basically of the contrasting colours of the white marble, pink Languedoc marble and golden stone used.

The building is laid out symmetrically on the courtyard side, asymmetrically on the garden side. Nothing obstructs the view towards the south and the Grand Canal. To the north stretches a perpendicular gallery, intended to protect the parterres against the wind. Another wing, Trianon-in-the-Woods, is hidden among the trees at right-angles. The idea of the peristyle joining the two wings of the palace sprang from the desire to preserve the panorama. This gallery was designed by Robert de Cotte, in the absence of Jules Hardouin-Mansart. On summer evenings, Louis XIV would organize balls or suppers, mostly reserved for a privileged few. Trianon is "a palace of marble, jasper and porphyry with delightful gardens". The marble and stone create a delicate harmony, continued in the flowers of the parterres.

We know that the spirit of the Versailles gardens originates in a whole mythological symbolism. At Trianon, none of this exists : the garden is a simple, though remarkable, homage to nature itself.

THE SMALL TRIANON

A privileged spot, the domain of Flora, the pleasure ground of Trianon always received the careful attention of the sovereigns of Versailles.

The "New Menagerie", completed by Gabriel in 1749, contains indigenous animals used for the selection of various species. It contains a farm, dovecot, hen-house, stable and dairy. To the east lies a new parterre, the French Garden.

In 1750, Gabriel erected the "French Pavilion" in the middle of this parterre. Its ground-plan is cross-shaped, with four cabinets surrounding a huge circular drawing-room adorned with a carved cornice representing farmyard animals. The Botanical Garden lies to the north.

In 1761, Madame de Pompadour suggested to Louis XV the construction of a small château in the French Garden. The project was entrusted to Gabriel, and in 1768, the Small Trianon was inaugurated. A masterpiece of neo-classical architecture, a model of harmony and refined elegance, the Small Trianon is Gabriel's most perfect creation. It has a square ground-plan, and includes a basement, a first floor and an attic surmounted by a balustrade.

In 1780, near the Small Trianon, Mique completed the construction of Marie-Antoinette's Theatre, skilfully hidden amongst the trees.

At present, only the first floor of the Small Trianon, where the 18th century décor has recently been restored, can be visited.

The wainscoting by Guibert has had its freshness restored. The paintings commissioned by Louis XV have been returned to the Dining-Room. In the Music Room, the triple-coloured damask, like that of the Queen's time, and the furniture, almost all of which was placed here by Empress Eugénie, conjure up that pleasantly simple art of living intrinsic to Trianon.

THE GARDENS
OF THE SMALL
TRIANON

On becoming mistress of
this domain in 1774, the
young Queen wished to
surround her palace with
new gardens in the Anglo-
chinese style, then in fash-
ion. A river issuing from a
lake runs through undulat-
ing lawns adorned with
rocks, rare species of trees
and several light construc-
tions.

In 1777, Richard Mique,
Marie-Antoinette's
architect, erected a small
octagonal pavilion, the
Belvedere, on a hillock
overlooking the Lake and,
on an islet in the river,
opposite the windows of
the Queen's chamber, a
round colonnade, with a
cupola, called the Temple of
Love. In the centre stands a
copy of a statue by
Bouchardon, "Love carving
his bow from Hercules'
club".

MARIE-ANTOINETTE'S
HAMLET

At the north-west end of
Trianon stands the famous
Hamlet, for which Mique
drew up the plans in 1783.
The Queen's Cottage,
linked with the Billiards
House by a wooden gallery,
stands among thickly-
leafed trees at the edge of a
lake. Nine thatched cot-
tages cluster around it,
including the Malborough
Tower, the dairy, the barn,
the dovecot, the mill, etc.
In this charming setting,
intended to be a real farm,
the Queen liked to imagine
she was leading a country
life and often stayed here
with her children and a few
friends.

61